ELBA JOURNAL

by

JILL BAKER

A Winchester Cottage Print Book

A Winchester Cottage Print Book

WinchesterCottage Print
A Division of Winchester Cottage Fine Art and Print
618 Main Street, #184
New Harmony, Indiana 47631

Printed in the United States of America

“ABLE WAS I ERE I SAW ELBA”

JULY 1, 1975

Today I began a journey to a small world, the micro-empire of Elba which now has the honor of being a summer resort and is the destination for thousands of Europeans searching for an unspoiled spa anywhere in the sun washed Mediterranean.

At Piombino Maritimo-on-the-Harbor, on the West Coast of Italy, my husband, a bearded college professor and writer, my two daughters, 3 and 7, and I (an ordinary- looking wife, mother and artist) boarded the big boat to sail across a small stretch of the Mediterranean. My heart beat faster, as we were now on our way to a new adventure. For three hours we stood in the spray at the rail and looked across the expanse of the Mediterranean. I love the sea and it was a pleasing thought that we would be near it or bathing in it for a whole month.

As we approached the island on this beautiful day, a flying fish sailed across the incredible blue-green water toward our boat. It was an omen, a welcome. The water far away, near the island, appeared black, though looking straight down I could clearly see fifty feet beneath the surface.

Elba seemed to rise suddenly from the sea, like two green

mountains growing out of the water. Tiny mirrors of the sun glinted on the shining black water among reflected flecks of pale green mountains. Tiny, pointed islands, some only a single rock, some made of many rocks, pierced the green shallows. Beyond them rose up not one, but the imposing bulk of two large mountains that make up the mainland of Elba.

The smell of the cold, salty sea was in the wind, with the froth that turned into a haze lying along the base of the towering cliffs facing us. As our ship drew near the rocky heights we saw that their sheer sides were uninhabitable. Fierce and dry; no house or road could ever have found a foothold on them. As we slid below them we entered the haze, and they loomed above us in the blinding blue-grey sky. White gulls flew out from rocks located somewhere in the fog, wheeling and crying as we passed into their shadow.

Sailing north, hugging the cliffy coast, we finally found an entrance and pulled into the harbor of Porto Ferraio. Here we disembarked and found ourselves in the center of the town. After a wait with a mixture of other travelers at the immigration gate, German tourists, Italian tourists, farmers and their families, we found our way onto an old, crowded bus which then roared and lumbered along for a half-hour, up over the central saddleback and down to the other side of the island; standing all the way. As the rickety bus began its cautious descent along the steep, curving highway on the South side of the island, we caught brief glimpses of blue bays and sailing ships on the sea ahead of us, brightly colored flowers and farmhouses in clean white shapes through the trees. On one side, high above us, was perched what looked like a castle on an impossible pyramid of a hill.

The bus wound down through the foothills and across the valley to the edge of the ocean, where it stopped. A little tired from our trip, we pulled our bags off the bus and looked around Marina di Campo. The square was shaded with umbrella pines and sparkling with flowers. My friend Luisa was there and greeted us happily, giving all of us hugs. She had come to meet us in her car to take us to our lodgings.

We found what is to be our home for a month one mile inland from the little fishing village of Marino di Campo. It is a farmhouse in the old style, which is one way to say it is an efficient, thick-walled building, built to house both man and beasts, so that humans live on the upper floor, which is alternately warmed by the animals in the winter or cooled by the winds that pass through the high windows or the stable-barn below in the summer.

On the back side of this whitewashed building, facing the driveway, are broad white steps leading up to the back porch, the only entrance to the house, which is located on the second floor. We were shown around the house by our new landlords, an old farmer, Dino Guido, and his wife, Emelda. I can speak Italian enough to understand only part of what they are saying in their country dialect, which is hard enough for Luisa to understand, and she is Italian, born in Florence.

The size of the living area is just right for the needs of our family for one month. There is a large kitchen just inside the door, a central sitting or dining room beyond it, where a large dining table is set up, with two bedrooms and a bath opening off of it. The owners, the farmer and his wife, live next door in a tiny, new house, a square wooden box much less imaginative than their old farm building. Behind these two buildings are smaller, crumbling out-buildings, housing chickens, goats, and rabbits. A donkey lives below us in the barn, along with dark rooms full of stored potatoes and farm implements. Already many cats and two dogs have welcomed us and we have praised the farmer's wife for the flowers and vegetables that she grows in her rather large garden.

After opening our bags I could hardly wait to explore the village and the beach, where I hope to spend most of my time this summer. My husband elected to remain in the house, so the two girls and I rode with Luisa the mile back to the village. Luisa walked around with us while we shopped, showing us where the shops are and telling us what to buy and what kind of sunscreen to use.

The little town of Maritimo di Campo da Lucia has only one main road, which curves around the small, blue bay, lined with shops. I bought beach toys, some of the beautiful fruits and vegetables that are temptingly displayed on sidewalk stands and bread hot from the oven at the forneria for our lunch, some of which we ate on the white, sandy beach. My daughters got to play in the gritty sand and dance in the pale blue shallows until they got their skirts wet.

Luisa told me that her mother, whom I have not yet met, is excited, more excited than she has ever seen her in her life. She is getting a new grand piano and it was delivered today. She will play it after it is tuned, and the piano tuner is arriving with the piano, so she will be able to play it this afternoon. For though Luisa was happy we had arrived, she seemed even more preoccupied with her mother's good fortune.

Luisa seemed strangely tense and nervous about the arrival of the piano and was anticipating going back to the penthouse apartment to see the piano and her mother. So we left Luisa at the townhouse, where she is staying with her mother and her children and we three, my two girls and I, walked two kilometers along the dusty road leading away from the bay, back to our house, carrying our loot in net bags.

Since we were walking, I was able to look at the valley we live in from the road. The valley stretches back from the bay inland. Above us, on the green hills around the flat valley, perch ancient villages. And above them rise the even higher mountains, dark green at first, turning rocky and black, treeless and impenetrable. As we ambled home, the sun beat down on us, piercing hot, yet invisible in the haze.

Back at the farmhouse, my daughters scratched in the dirt with their tiny new rakes and shovels, petted the little gray donkey and cried when the tomcat climbed a tree and stole a baby bird for supper. Tired from their travels, they went to bed willingly enough tonight.

They have come a long way today, their tired little bodies having been carried from Florence to this farmhouse located on a water-bound bit of rock out in the Mediterranean Ocean by train, boat, bus, car and foot, from daybreak till dark. Now they trustingly lie in a new bed, too tired to worry about where in the world they are. They do not understand the unique place in the world in which they sleep, surrounded by an ocean named "The Center of the Earth."

JULY 2

Last night I discovered that there are killer mosquitoes on this island. They are as large as mayflies and their bites are as big around as quarters! Since Italians have never heard of putting screens in their windows, I will have to close the windows at night, no matter how stuffy it gets.

After being awakened by the first bite, I lay awake listening for the high-pitched whine that would signal a second attack. What I heard were cars drumming by occasionally on the road, the donkey stamping below us, the refrigerator humming, dogs barking far away and, finally the roosters crowing before the sun rose. It seems quiet in the country, but there are lots of noises.

I am astounded by the brilliant colors. I do not know why they are so much brighter here on Elba, probably because of the clear air, free from any kind of pollution. We are too far out at sea to be bothered by any mainland factories or too many car exhausts. We saw the incredible colors as we walked the sunny dusty road to town today, the two girls and I. Really red poppies, very green corn, blue, purple and pink windflowers, yellow ginestre, white daisies and lilies in many shades of orange. In the trees hung peaches or cherries as translucent as rubies, figs, and grapes as small and green as peas. In the field, grasses hung out their miniature oriental lamps or purple plumes with a load of seeds. Lizards, brown and dry, slipped from beneath our feet and rushed noisily into the weeds. The grey haze hung over our head until noon, when the sky suddenly appeared, a dazzling baby blue over mounds of white clouds.

This afternoon, Luisa and her children came to the farm where we are staying and we grown-ups sat in the shade on the patio in front of Dino Guido's small white house while our four children played about the farmyard. Luisa had brought her dark-haired girl and blond boy, aged six and four. We sat across the table from our farmer-landlord and listened to him talking in simple Italian to Luisa. Dino's speech was so basic that even I could understand him as he served my husband, Luisa and me generous glasses of his homemade wine. Luisa translated: "Pliny the Elder, even long ago in Roman days, called Elba 'The Island of the good wine.'"

Dino's brown face, puffed and stubbly, is younger than the 66 years he claims. A strong odor of old sweat exuded from him from time to time. He appears both young and ancient, wise and ignorant. He was fearful and shy yesterday when we arrived, but today, knowing our names and bolstered by his wine, he was happy and polite and eager to impress us. His hands moved in animated expressions of what he wants to convey to us, as if they were the only thing we could understand. He spoke proudly of his daughters and his one son and the vegetables he grows. He spoke of the poor prices he got for his crops. He pressed more of his wine on us, and then more when we had finished that. The wine he served was thick, rich and sweet. He was happy to have plenty of it and wanted to see us enjoy it and warm to him.

I speak little Italian, though I understand a lot I hear. But Luisa is Italian and knows the island and the people well, having come here every summer since she was a child. Her conversation flowed as freely as Dino's wine. At last, interrupted by our children and the arrival of the farmer's pregnant daughter, we rose and moved into the depths of the dark, cool barn to look over and buy fresh beans and zucchini from the farmer's wife. She weighed them on an antique hand-held scale before putting them in baskets. She motioned us to follow her back along a narrow, well-trod path through the tall weeds, past the chicken-house, past the rabbit shed to the edge of the field where the cherry tree drooped its fruit-laden branches to the ground. Standing in one spot, I pulled off enough cherries to make two pies, putting them all in a basket the farmer's wife brought me.

With the little stock of pans I found in the kitchen, I made two cherry pies in my tiny oven. I rolled out the white dough with a cup and settled it in a pan, then dumped the beautiful, red cherries into it. With sugar, butter, a little lemon juice and a top crust, I completed my first pie and began making the second. They both would not fit in the oven until I gathered some rocks to prop up a bottom shelf I found and put the two pies on different levels.

The farmer's wife received the offering of one of the pies at her door and a dubious look broke through her usually unexpressive face. Behind her, the old farmer smiled and tried to make me come in the house, but the farmer's wife stood in the door, shielding her house from my view. Her thin, work-hardened body was now clothed in clean layers of calico. She had never seen an American pie and I explained what it was. I do not recall seeing anything like it here in Europe, or anything that resembles it for size and sweetness.

We ate our pie for dessert and its familiar, tart taste brought back memories of visiting relatives in the South when I was growing up. I wondered if the Italian family next door was enjoying their pie tonight.

JULY 3

The children and I got up when the day began to warm, put on our bathing suits and over them light clothes that covered every part of our bodies for our walk in the sun, per Luisa's directions. We gathered the beach toys, some water to drink and set out. I will buy something in the village to bring home for our lunch and supper every day. My husband chooses to stay in the house and write. In spite of my urging and disappointment that he does not want to go, he will not walk with us to the beach.

Rimming the bay, the beach is bordered with a low wall,

places to eat and a broad sidewalk. The sidewalk is long and curves along the crescent beach, all white and pink with bodies. Germans are in abundance. You hear many languages spoken, and English is almost always understood. If they do not understand English I speak in halting Italian.

The clear, hot sun is the enemy here, though people lie around in it and bare their children's bodies on purpose for a tan. However, the shade trees bordering the beach are welcome to me, and I wear a large hat when I've exposed myself to the sun for the allotted amount of time. Luisa has given me the times I am allowed to go out each day, so that the children and I will not overexpose ourselves immediately, like so many people do. We are beginning with only a small amount of exposure.

When we reached the sidewalk by the beach, the girls and I turned to the left and trekked in our sandals all the way down it to the very far end of the beach, where the nice bathhouses are spaced out evenly near the clean, white sand, in the exclusive area. There Luisa and her two already very tan boy and girl, had already set up their chairs on the beach. Luisa sits with her mother in a spot where her eyes can watch the children without a second's lapse, as they bathe, running in and out of the water's edge, laughing and playing with other naked children.

My children look different from the others because they wear bathing suits. Somehow I can not rid myself of the Victorian ethic where my daughters are concerned. And, even though I admire them, I can not bring myself to wear the barely-there hand-crocheted bikinis that some grown women are wearing. My grandmother would have called them handmade doilies.

I sat with Luisa and her thin, white-haired mother, whom I met here for a brief moment yesterday and we talked awhile. She spoke slowly in an elegant, carefully enunciated Italian so that I realized that she must be a little drunk. Though she spoke only of the beach and the weather. I felt myself drawn to her, and though I could not see her darting eyes behind the dark glasses, she exuded a hidden sense of longing, yearning for something I did not understand. I put it down to the fact that she was Italian and a member of a past generation, and I therefore could not comprehend her experiences.

The children finished bathing, we dressed them in their little shorts outfits and Luisa and I walked up and down the beach with them. As we walked and talked, we gazed distractedly at the myriad body types we saw exposed, a constant source of entertainment for the subconscious mind. There are bodies that are tanned and lean, others are white and bloated, men and women, some young, some old, some handsome, some ugly, dressed in all kinds of dishabille.

But for the most part, Luisa and I were intent on our discussion of life and its complexities. Every day we catch the other up on what has occurred in our life overnight and our thoughts about it. We are both convinced we know the solutions to the other's problems if only they would act on our suggestions. Luisa is concerned about her mother, who has so many expectations of this summer. She is afraid she will be disappointed.

At noon, I packed the girls' toys and clothes up and we began our walk back home, along the way stopping at the fruit and vegetable stands and the forneria for some meat to eat when we get home.

The dry, scalding heat here on Elba was almost too much for me this morning. The walk back from the beach at 1:00, the hottest part of the day, a two-kilometer trek, herding two small, tired children along a busy road, carrying heavy bags of groceries, was an ordeal. I tell myself that it is too much trouble to go all the way to the far end of the beach to swim with Luisa, but it is true that there my children can play with hers without a crowd around and we have the convenience of Luisa's bath house in which to change clothes and shower.

The farm that we've become a part of, on the other hand, grows more and more enjoyable. This afternoon the girls squealed with delight upon seeing a goat being milked by the farmer's wife, and were allowed to lead the baby goat into the pasture. I discovered some kind of carved wooden seat that is placed on the donkey's back to carry firewood, with a dusty, ancient bicycle propped against it and a round wicker basket which the farmer's wife uses for gathering potatoes. All together they made up a country still-life beside the barn. They were all so typical and gray that I began to sketch them.

The farmer's wife came out while I was drawing them and picked up the basket, right in the middle of my sketching. She used it to gather pears that had fallen during the hard "pentoso" that began blowing this afternoon. She brought a bunch to me and placed them on the bench beside me. "Per lei," (For you) she said. I asked her if they had eaten the pie I had made and she frankly said that it was too sweet, they could not eat it. I wondered what they had done with it. But she turned and went away.

The wind rattles the windows and roars in the dining room chimney. It blows fruit down onto the roof and ruffles the chickens' feathers so that they finally run to huddle in the shed. It blows away the haze that has lain on the hills and reveals a clear-cut horizon of hills overlapping in layers against a flat, blue sky. Now you can see buildings far away on the ridges and the black pattern on the high hillside where the woods burned last year. The farmer said he leads his donkey up those hills in the winter to gather firewood. We notice that there is no way to heat our apartment, except with the fireplace, and the Guidos must have lived here during the winters.

Inside, with my husband, I begin to squirm under his anxious, silent glare, feeling guilty because I have spent so much money on food today in the village. He has been at home fretting and writing all day. A professor without a class, a writer without an audience, the author of five books that have yet to be published, and full of nervous frustration, he is like a pressure cooker with a tight lid, about to blow. He wonders out loud why his life is so full of sharp declines and so few happy pinnacles. I stepped out on the porch.

I decided, before the sun went down, to take a walk along

the dirt road that runs around the valley, over the foothills and into town. It wandered past gardens and passed beside white walls. A house stood by a field, its plaster walls crumbling at the corners to reveal long logs that formed the sub-structure, overlapping like those of an American log cabin. The fields of rich wheat were blowing in the wind. Grape fields and peach orchards all seem very small, compared to the seas of crops and orchards that I am used to in the United States, but these are of the correct proportion to feed a family.

Gradually, the fields gave way to walled gardens, rock paths and steps climbing upward to well-kept homes. As I came closer to the town of Marino di Campo, the buildings became crowded and old, with thick-leafed, low trees waving around them. Beneath one of them I saw an old well, the pulley still on it. Rumple-stockinged women with square bodies and coarse black hair watched me curiously as they passed, carrying their loads or walking arm in arm with a man.

Then young men began to enter the street as it went down toward the central square, walking to town, looking for entertainment. They gathered in brightly-colored flocks at the corners. They watched me with measuring eyes as I passed and posed themselves in welcoming postures. Some spoke in low voices to me as I passed, saying things in Italian that I did not understand. It made me nervous.

In the square I turned to the right, passing the varnished fishing boats in the marine harbor, on my way to the distant quay. Rising above it is a small, cylindrical tower which was built as part of a defense system, probably for the duration of Pisan rule, which I hoped to explore, but the gate leading to its path was locked.

The sound of the sea was everywhere around me, as evening fell. The sky was turning pink and gray; mare's tail clouds whipped across it. Standing on the quay, I looked out to the blue-black sea. Below me were huge, round rocks. The wind made fan patterns on the surface of the water as it blew through the rocks. A feeling of sadness fell on me as I watched a single star in the cool sky turning yellow. From here the mighty hills were only torn black paper on frosted glass. I turned and went back to the farm, trying to reach it before it was completely dark.

After cleaning up the kitchen at midnight, I turned off the lights and stepped out on the back porch again, this time into absolute darkness. There were no outside lights anywhere on the farm. Only a few distant homes had lights. The air, the sky, everything was totally black. As I stood there, the stars began to appear, the bright ones first. Soon my eyes could see a vast array above—small and large stars—the galaxies in orderly gyrations, shining in the sky. There were more stars than I had ever seen. The sky seemed brilliant with light and the light from the stars lighted the earth so that I could make out the shapes of the hills and houses around me. The depth and beauty of an experience I had had in childhood came back to me, with the memory of one night, camping out with my sisters. On that night, as I lay on my back gazing into the heavens, I could see shooting stars, comets and falling stars by the dozens, and thought it was a nightly event which I had missed by living in the city.

Civilization and towns have always drowned the night sky with light for me and from that time until tonight, I have not been far enough from lights to see all those stars lying open in a windy sky.

JULY 4

Today we passed the middle point of the year. The first half, spent in Florence, is over and has become a section of time to cut and paste in a photo album. Only this month in Italy remains before we return to the United States and to our familiar language, home and neighbors. Yet here we still remain in Italy, in the last episode of a dream from which I shall awaken. What we are doing here I do not know. I only know that when our six-month lease ran out in Florence, we had an extra month to spend in Italy and nowhere to spend it. My newly-made and now very dear friend, Luisa, from Florence, offered and then insisted on finding us a place to stay on the island of Elba so that we could remain near her and her children a little bit longer.

At last, being on Elba is becoming a reality and I'm just beginning to realize where I am. The pattern of the days is becoming routine: the early morning sun, the white beach with Luisa, her children and sometimes her mother until noon, the long afternoon nap, the evening "passeagiato", the wind rising with the coming of dark at 10:00 and the final sound of grass blowing outside our rooms as I fall asleep.

I found out soon that the mosquitoes will not bite us at night if we are slathered with baby oil, which I originally put on the children's skin before they went to bed only to counteract the effects of the sun. Now I know it keeps the mosquitoes from eating us for most of the night.

The fact that we are on an island is all too real to my husband, who worries about it, feeling trapped. It was easy to get here, he says, but getting off is another question. His anxieties were partially relieved when I reported that I had seen a bus and boat schedule in the central piazza which listed frequent departures.

Luisa is rather insistent on running our affairs, but she is also wise and realizes when she has told me once too often what to do, and apologizes with the statement "I guess I forget that you have just as much experience as I do." She is one year older than I, yet I feel older. She is undisciplined in her own life, but controlling of others'. She has childish whims, such as insisting that her children bathe naked, though they ask for bathing suits like my children have. She must have her way or she gets angry. She is packed with energy and I admit that she is good with children.

I like Luisa and enjoy talking with her, but I have to ignore her demands at times. Even my three-year-old looks at her with mature, questioning eyes when she asks too much. I wish I were closer to her, as we sometimes become during our conversations, because I would like to help her grow to her full potential. She is actually very intelligent and knowledgeable in many fields. But the things that are important to her are manners, money and getting lots of attention, the very things she says she does not care about.

During the day, Luisa and I run along the beach in our bikinis and sit in the sun on our lounge chairs, groggily watching the tiny bottoms of naked children diving in the blue sea. We hear Luisa's mother in her big straw hat, who has already drunk too much by 11:00, talking to herself with gentilesse. Luisa commands her children to do something. My children recount their small adventures in great detail to me and I am humming a tune. We are all in our own little worlds, no matter how hard we try to break into each other's. A flock of gulls wheels in the blue sky. Grey clouds scud along behind them and the fishing boats with their sails full of wind are drawn by invisible forces into the distant black of the Mediterranean.

JULY 5

We rode the bus into town today instead of walking. The roads through the little village are very narrow; just wide enough for two cars to pass. Besides the traffic lanes, there is a parking lane on one side. When our big bus lumbered through the town we had to stop half-way down one of the blocks. My oldest daughter and I were standing in the front because it was so crowded. My youngest was sitting on a generous woman's lap. A tiny white station wagon had stalled in one of the lanes and had been abandoned there. Other cars might have been able to pass, but our big bus could not squeeze between it and the parked cars on the right. People in sunglasses stepped out of the shops to peer at our predicament when they saw the street was empty of traffic. The bus driver and his helper got out of the bus to wander up and down the street on the pretense of finding the driver of the station wagon but in reality stretching their legs. No horns were blown as the cars began to pile up behind us. No one on the bus got excited. Everyone settled back and enjoyed the unexpected respite until the driver of the station wagon came back with an apologetic grin to move it. Everyone returned to their places and the bus continued on its way to the beach.

Luisa and I sat on our beach chairs in the blazing sun watching the children running about to find interesting rocks. Luisa's mother was having one of her more lucid days. She is a large woman, but very thin, sinking into her loose skin, pale, almost blue under the enormous straw hat that she ties on with a checkered bandanna under her chin.

"I heard the lizards singing this morning," she suddenly said. She was speaking in Italian and in a voice so low that I was not sure that she was speaking to me, the only one sitting beside her. When I looked at her she turned her head ever so slightly and I saw by the twinkle in her eye that she knew what I was thinking.

"Lizards?" I said, sending my 3-year-old off down the beach to catch up with the bigger children in her new bathing panties. I gazed at the mother's white hands, carefully kept in the shade of the beach umbrella over her. They were large and white and faintly dotted. The tendons and muscles showed they had once been powerful – they were pianist's hands. With age they had become soft and flaccid, the muscles wasted, the bones white, showing through the thin film of skin.

"The pirates' lizard canaries." She explained, gazing into the distance, her eyes squinting as if seeing something that I could not see. "A long time ago a Spanish pirate ship carrying canaries was wrecked on the rocks to the Southwest, off that way." and one long arm waved vaguely in the direction of the boardwalk down the beach. "Many of the canaries were freed when the cages were smashed on the rocks and they flew over here, to Elba. Now they are called lizard canaries. What an ugly name for such a beautiful bird."

"I've never seen one. What do they look like?" I asked, amazed at this rare conversation with a woman who had hardly spoken two words to me since my arrival on the island.

"They are green," she said, tipping her head back and closing her eyes to see them better. "Greenish-yellow. Actually they shine like brass or silver and have gold on the tips of their feathers. They look like they have coins pasted all over their bodies, like scales, I suppose. Their feet are dark, not yellow, like real canaries' feet. On their heads is a little oval cap of bright orange. They sing like heaven, like a mockingbird. Sometimes I hear them in the mornings." She looked at me for a moment, slowly, with one eye, to see if I believed her. I was silent, wondering if I should. Her eye closed. After a few moments of silence I thought she had fallen asleep again and rose to leave. As I did, I saw one long, slender hand glide under the folds of her big, white beach towel, which lay over and hid the bottle of gin.

My baby and I had gotten sunburned, we so tried not to spend too much time in the sun today. But I let my oldest daughter play out in the sun and now she is burned. Thank goodness it is only a mild burn. Luisa says that novice sunbathers here can and do actually blister, the sun is so direct and the air so absolutely clear out here in the middle of the sea.

The water is clear too, cold and transparent, and I was shocked at the lack of sea life. I've seen no small fishes and we have found hardly any shells on this beach. The sand is made up of small grains of clear stone, agates. It is all very strange and different to me. I'm used to the coastal beaches of the United States, with all their shells and sea life.

The girls and I bought a crab at the fish market on our way home from the beach at noon. He was huge. With his long legs he was so big that when it came to cooking him I did not have a pot big enough. I borrowed one from the farmer's wife and set about the project with all kinds of advice from the excited children. Once it was cooked, we sat down to supper in the dining room. The girls and I enjoyed cracking the shells and eating the rich meat dipped in butter, but my husband, after a few half-hearted attempts at eating something which had been so recently alive, abandoned us. It was hard to eat with his disgust brooding over us. This should be fun, I thought. So when he left the table I tried to make it a party and the girls and I ate and stacked the empty shells in mounds while we laughed and talked about our day.

After supper I cleaned out the large shell off the back of the crab and hung it on the porch to dry in the sun to a bright orange. If it lasts, I will take it back to the States. It could be used for a bowl or a decoration.

Perhaps my husband is already thinking about our return to the U.S. He says he is worried about our house, which we rented to two students while we are traveling. Just after we left they accidentally injured our dog, which they had agreed to care for. But there was nothing we could do so far from home, and the dog recovered. I think about the house too, planning some remodeling. But my feeling is that as long as the house is still standing when we get back, I'll be happy.

Umbrella Pines

JULY 6

I was making another sketch of the potato basket. In the silence of the morning I could hear voices speaking in the distance in rapid Italian, though I could not make out the words. I pulled myself up from the rush-bottomed chair which was threatening to leave permanent waffle patterns on the back of my bare legs and looked down the road.

I saw an old, fat man with his old, fat wife walking along through the powdered dirt. The wife wore a black print dress. The man wore a white cap pulled down over his eyes, a white shirt and blue shorts. They were both waving their arms and speaking rapidly at the same time. Every few steps they would stop and face each other and talk even louder, with their hands gesturing even more emphatically, then resume their walk, side by side, still talking. The man was pointing in one direction, the woman, with a red purse flying from her hand, would point another way. Then they would stop and both point another way altogether. At a point about 50 feet from me they stopped in the center of the road, turned around and started walking back the way they had come, pausing to speak in rapid Italian, gesturing as wildly as before, from time to time. They disappeared behind a distant farmhouse, but I could hear their conversation continuing on and on, carried back to me on the hot breeze.

Later in the morning Luisa's immediate family of three and all four of mine jammed into one tiny car and climbed high up the side of a 1019-meters-high mountain until we reached the place where a small town balanced on the summit of one of its peaks. Near this ancient village of San Ilario, we three grown-ups (Luisa had sat between my husband and me in the front seat) and our four children got out of the cramped car and walked the rest of the way. There could be no cars in the center of town because there were no roads, only walkways and stairways of stone climbing up and down the impossibly steep hills between houses. The mountain wind was suddenly stilled in the curving, narrow passageways. Full of sun, they were sheltered and warm. Thick plaster walls of yellow, red tile roofs, stone block steps and walks of grey granite, iron railings of various curving designs – everything was picturesque. But the most amazing surprises were the flowers and plants. In pots, growing out of the rocks themselves, they grew in the bright sun to enormous size, abundance and variety – bougainvillea, geraniums, begonias, many flowers I recognized but cannot name. They astounded me with their dimension. The leaves, the stalks, the blooms of each familiar plant were two or three times the ordinary size, and their colors were much brighter. San Ilario is a most unusually blessed town.

We looked down from an open square at the top of the peak and beyond the peninsula at one end of the island all the way to the western sea. Today the sky was too hazy to see Corsica or Monte Cristo, usually visible from here, but we could see the valley below us and to the south, clearly, cupping the harbor town of Marino di Campo or Campo nell'Elba, from whence we had come. I saw the bay stretching into the valley, the houses of the village, the highway coming toward us and, finally could make out in miniature clarity, our little house on the farm of Dino Guido, like a doll's house set in the middle of a child's play yard with the late afternoon sun lighting it from a low angle. From our perspective, it was a child's toy house and we were giant children.

JULY 7

Coming from Florence to visit us for the week-end is our friend, a pleasant, single, blond American woman. Looking at our island through her eyes, the sand was almost too clean, the water too clear, the air so sweet it was not real. The only sign that we were on a beach and not in a painting was the sand in our eyebrows and the faint taste of salt in our hair when the wind whipped it into our mouths.

With her I snorkeled, floating on the surface and seeing the bay through the glass of my mask, watching the colored rocks glimmering up at me, patterned individually like the watercolors that my baby makes when I turn her loose on the floor with paints and paper. Cool colors faded into one another, gentle driftings and lines. The black rocks, their edges plunging in haphazard angles into the deeper, darker water, lay off the point. I opened my eyes and floated over them and their paler brother rocks lying half-buried in the sand of the bottom. Wavy kelp drifted like drowned maidens' hair upon them. Dark, sleek shapes skirted about them, over the white sand, darting and diving in fluid movements. Fish appeared to be plentiful in the deep water outside the bay.

I floated on my back, my eyes watching gray clouds gathering in packs on the giant hills. But the sun stopped them from coming any closer to us, burning them away before they reached the shore. The mighty winds that propelled them died on the jagged mountaintops when they met the harsh sun on the south side of the island and only a few little clouds were left in gasps to wisp away through the empty blue sky above me.

My husband came to the beach with us today for the first time, probably because our blond friend is so beautiful. Drying myself on the sand beside his pale body after snorkeling, I watched the even tenderer, pinker body of a tiny German boy trudging along beyond him. Naked and blond, he clutched a shovel and boat in his arms to ensure himself he would be entertained today. He marched fearlessly past the huge grown-ups, peering at us at every other step with one eye closed, searching for danger signals in our faces. He tramped past us down the beach, then turned and tramped back up it, following the trail of his older siblings with puffing determination.

I heard Luisa laughing at something my husband said. She joined us, but has spent more time talking to my husband than to my girlfriend, who was catching me up on the latest news about our mutual friends in Florence.

Out on the water, a tiny boater in a tiny boat paddled back and forth with his oar flashing, like the pink boy. Closer to shore, my oldest daughter was determinedly learning how to swim. Her feet were kicking behind her in the white froth of the edge, her short, dark hair curled over her cheeks as she struggled valiantly to make progress in the churning, unpredictable liquid. My baby, only three, mimicked her, standing on her hands in the shallows, her feet floating behind her and her blond hair dribbling like a mermaid's around her blue, laughing eyes. She is lighter and quicker in the water, and seemed more akin to a slim, blue fish that rippled in a nearby current, than to her sister.

By noonday, the blazing sun and the blue, hazy sea were just the right color to distinctly set off the distant sailboats drifting and the white yachts at anchor. My husband left to go home, taking the children, afraid of the sun. I spent the rest of the day showing my friend the sights of the town, though she was more interested in the men. We ate lunch, shopped, and returned to the beach. She is determined to get as much out of her day as she can, as she returns tomorrow morning to the mainland.

We could hear the faint sound of music bouncing over the water from the dockside cafe on the far side of the bay. We silently moved toward it like dreamers in the heat, past closed shops and through empty streets, aware that the sun-darkened bodies of Italians were napping just behind the closed shutters we passed.

JULY 8

Luisa's father arrived in Elba yesterday. This morning he sat far from us while we were bathing at the beach, up by the bath house with his silent wife, in the beach chairs. When Luisa invited my husband, my friend and me up to the beach house to meet him, I saw he had almost white hair and a still youthful face. Closer yet, I saw that he did not look his 58 years. His lean, stern face smiled only briefly to be polite, then closed up forbiddingly. His well-toned body, that he believes will carry him to his 150th year, was tan. A small towel was wrapped about the upper half of his left arm and pinned to cover an old wound. Luisa said it was the first time she had ever seen him without a shirt in the presence of people other than his family.

Luisa's father had been in an accident the year before he met her mother and the muscles had been torn off the top of his left arm. Luckily, that was the year that they brought penicillin into Italy and when they injected it into his swollen body he survived. Her mother, who at the time was already hailed in Rome as a promising concert pianist, became infatuated with the handsome young man, who, being a lawyer, was a desirable bachelor and rapidly becoming very wealthy. They married in Rome, uniting two old, well-to-do Roman families. When their first child, Luisa, was born a year later the new father demanded that Luisa's mother either give up her piano or give up the child. She was in despair, knowing she had no choice in the matter. The piano was moved out of the house.

Luisa grew to be like her father, powerful, active, dark-haired and willful. Then her younger brother was born. Her mother stopped bearing children because of his difficult birth and began to supervise a series of moves from house to house in different parts of Italy as her husband grew in power and wealth. Moving to a very large house in Florence when Luisa was fifteen, they finally settled down and made the formal series of visits that would be their initiation into the social life of the city. The father had big plans for his daughter. The second child, the son, had turned out to be artistic, blond, passive and quiet, like his mother. But the forceful, intelligent personality of the daughter was a perfect companion to the influential attorney. He trained her to work in his office and made plans for her to enter law school.

However, Luisa's greatest interest was in languages. She began college in Florence as her father wished, but in the second year she requested to be allowed to attend the Sorbonne in Paris.

Her father said she could attend for only one semester, thinking he would indulge her with this one request temporarily. However, while in Paris, she met a brilliant Chinese man, also a linguist, and they became close friends. I suspect they fell in love, though she never said so. In spite of her pleading to remain in Paris, her father hastily brought her back to Florence, fearing that she would marry the man.

Once back in Florence, Luisa found her father had arranged for her to marry one of her cousins, someone from her own social class. She met her cousin, David, at a formal dinner party set up for the occasion, and they were chaperoned at many social functions while he courted her during the days that followed. David's weak, pallid personality appalled her and that fact, along with her tempestuous pronouncements, forced her family to agree that he was no match for her.

At a party soon after the failure of that union, she met a tall, dark-haired young man, someone very mature for his young age. Dominico was handsome, intelligent, reserved, aloof, and somewhat of a playboy. Luisa was immediately attracted to him and he to her. They met several times at various events. She learned that he was the son and only heir of a factory owner who had placed him at the age of eighteen in the position of accountant and manager of his plant. His education was not scholarly, but practical and certainly well-suited for the position he was destined to fill. Though he was Noveau Riche and from a family not quite as wealthy as Luisa's, his family had status enough in the city of Florence. Her parents agreed that, provided they fulfill a three-year engagement period, they could marry. The time passed and they married when Luisa was twenty.

Luisa had been married for three years, occupying her time with finishing her degree and helping her husband in the factory when the floods of 1966 arrived. The young couple awoke one morning to find that the entire factory had been washed down the river in the flood. Suddenly they were penniless and entirely dependent on Luisa's father. The loss of the factory killed Dominico's father.

As Luisa's father could no longer summon up any respect for a man with no education and now no wealth, he began to despise and belittle Luisa's husband to her, trying to regain control of his daughter. It was an effort made easier by their monetary dependence on him.

Luisa's father owns several homes in Italy. One of them is

the penthouse here on Elba, a block from the beach, where her mother always comes to spend the summer. Luisa comes to spend one month during the summer with her mother. Sometimes her father comes to visit on the weekends. When he arrives, according to Luisa, the normally relaxed household routine becomes unbearably tense. The best china and linens must be used at all meals; children must remain silent and behave properly during these meals. The house must be kept absolutely quiet and completely spotless at all times.

After all those years, Luisa's mother decided at the end of last summer, that she had had enough. When she returned from Elba, she told her husband she wanted a separation and moved into a hotel in Florence. Then, in the late fall, she came to spend a month in Elba with Luisa and the children, and Luisa spent a miserable month while a battle ensued between her separated parents. At the end of the month Luisa's mother acquiesced and moved back into her husband's house in Florence. But defeat had changed her. She had given up. Her health deteriorated and she began to depend on alcohol or sedatives to keep going. She did nothing all day but sit in front of the mirror and mourn. Then she began to visit Luisa's house, where she intruded upon Luisa's already stressful family life, hoping to find a reason to live.

She befriended Dominico's widowed mother and the two women went places together, visiting their children or shopping.

It appears to me that this summer Luisa's mother is living in a state of constant inebriation. However, in this sunny climate she at least makes an effort to partake of healthy food and to venture out into the sun every day. She seemed to be getting a little healthier and happier, at least until yesterday.

Luisa told me that at the beginning of the month she had moved a piano into the penthouse, but her muscles had atrophied after so many years of neglecting her art. Her mind could not bear the strain of hearing the music come out so halting and weak and now she had stopped trying to play, as it was too agonizing for her discriminating ear. At the end of the week she found her tears falling on the keys as she played, mourning over the decades of pleasure lost and the destruction of her ability to play the beautiful music she loved. She had given up trying to play after that.

Though Luisa managed to avoid all contact with her father throughout the day yesterday, she said when she went home last night he had surprised her by offering to take her children to the circus. This was a special treat for the children that he had never done before. Maybe he senses he has pushed his family as far as he can and is attempting to win them back.

Luisa's younger brother is just completing his exams at the University of Florence in engineering. He had given up trying to be an artist and had entered a more practical field to please the family. He is 24 years old and is in the process of being divorced. He is only slightly ambitious, in Luisa's estimation and is more the quiet, steady, plodding type. Luisa says that, if he is lucky, he may become a professor at the University after a long time, unless another aspirant on his pushy way to the top elbows him out of the race. I personally believe that he will make professor with his father's money and prestige, as that seems to weigh more in what it takes to become a professor in the Italian university system.

JULY 9

I find myself living in either water, dust or sand. The sand is everywhere, in my clothes, in the water, in the dust, on the beach. The dust, fine and white, settles on everything—on the sides of the long road we walk to town and back, turning the grass, the flowers and the trees white. I live in the water, swimming twice a day and then bathing to get the salt off my skin at night. It is in my ears at all times, in the damp towels and bathing suits I hang out to dry on the back porch by the big red crab shell.

As we walked the long road together today my oldest daughter told me in great detail what she would do with my body after I die. She will dress me in white satin and flowers and put me in a glass case in a glass room where she can see me every day. I was quiet while she talked on and on. My feelings were mixed. I love her for wanting to see me and honor me in my glass coffin every day, for her saying she will pray for me every day. Yet on the other hand, it seems strange that she imagines me dead.

I know where she gets her ghoulish ideas. She gets them from the holy relics we saw in such abundance in the great cathedrals all over Italy, where the realistically painted, elaborately dressed images of the saints are laid in glass cases. The church in Sienna has the actual head of St. Katherine in a little glass box for all to see when they enter. I feel disgust at the idea of my poor, used-up body being stared at when I am no longer conscious. Recognition at that point will not make any difference to me.

By keeping a respectful attitude toward the relics I have allowed her imagination to do what a typical seven-year-old's mind would do with such monstrosities as dried out saints, overly ornate chapels, banks of candles, golden frames and flowers everywhere. She peoples her chapels with the ones she loves, and says she prays, in her childlike way, for a beautiful home in heaven for me, cleaned by the angels, with angels to help me because they do not have anything else to do. Maybe this is because I have been stressing the importance of keeping the house clean lately.

Both children long to go back home to the United States. But I doubt that they will be much better off. I'm afraid I have been tense here, with all the things happening in Luisa's family and mine. I feel increasing unspoken pressures from my husband and I am hard on the children, trying to match Luisa's high expectations of their behavior. Her children speak English, but mine can not play with anyone else because they do not speak Italian. Their restriction to the apartment in Florence was the equivalent of a hypothetical restriction to our yard at home. My oldest daughter was already getting in trouble when we left America for releasing penned-up dogs. In Florence she got in trouble for almost letting a rabbit destined to be dinner for some Italian family out of its cage. Her desire to pet little, furry animals is probably a desire for caresses I can not give her enough of.

She possesses a great curiosity and a desire not only to see everything going on around her but to understand it. She asks questions for which I have no answers. She often asks questions which I never even asked myself and therefore do not know the answer. If I can not answer, I will tell her "I don't know" and add, "perhaps that is one thing you can do research on when you grow up." One question, for instance, was "Why do the right and left sides of the brain control opposite sides of the body, rather than the right side controlling the right and the left the left?" Another question she asked was "What would happen if you put smallpox vaccine in a mouse's ear?" and "If a cow gets a stomach ache, is it only in one stomach?" I find it hard to answer her questions concerning imaginary scenarios.

JULY 13

Luisa talked to me some more on the beach today. All during her young married life she said her great desire was for many offspring and when she married she could not believe that her husband hated children. However, she also realized her desire to have children did conflict with her goals and major aims in life, so she and Dominico agreed that after they had been married for seven years, she would have children. She held him to this agreement and in the seventh year she promptly became pregnant without warning her husband she was going to do so.

When he found out, he was unhappy about it and became cool toward her. The pregnancy was painful and Luisa was continually beset by threats of losing the baby. Their dark-haired baby daughter finally arrived through a terrible and painful delivery. Somehow, though, in this child, Luisa at last felt that she had an ally against her husband and father. She no longer faced them alone. Buoyed up by the presence of the baby, she suddenly decided to do something she had always wanted to do. With her husband's grudging permission, she adopted a little blond boy, already three years old, nine months after her daughter was born.

With his continued coolness and displeasure at his home life, and aggravated by Luisa's father's harassment of him, Dominico began to escape by chasing other women. Finally, distressed over her husband's affairs, Luisa drove off in the camping vehicle with the children and stayed away from her husband for a month until he begged them to come home, with promises to love and care for them all. Luisa also decided to tell her father that she planned to move her family away from Florence in order to escape his stranglehold on their lives.

However, during this time in her life, a couple of medical problems cropped up to complicate things. Her adored adopted son showed signs of brain damage that Luisa had several doctors check out. Eventually she became reconciled to his condition, which was neither severe nor unalterable, as they said it might disappear with time.

Then, Luisa herself underwent a precarious operation for the removal of a loose bone above the bridge of her nose that threatened to wander into her brain. This was done successfully only when Luisa went by herself to the clinic of the best surgeon in Europe, in Switzerland, and sat waiting in his office for three days until he saw her and agreed to do the operation himself.

It had been through this same stubbornness that she acquired her son. The red tape, the denial of her presence and the endless petitioning that are characteristic of the usual slow, chaotic Italian bureaucracy were forced to give in to her aggressive and persistent desires.

She has been married now for twelve years. Once, as a gift, her father assigned all the profits of a small boutique he owns in Florence to her. Through the years she has carefully hoarded these sums in a savings account.

Her husband is now a successful salesman of medical equipment and has learned to give in to most of her demands, though grudgingly. He spends most of his time away from home, either in the city or out of town, selling in his district of Tuscany. He has always wanted to own a sailboat and sail around the world. He spends many of his summer weekends with a sailor friend or helping with sailing regattas. Luisa gets dreadfully seasick whenever she gets on a boat, so Dominico has never been able to consider buying a boat for the family. When I visited Dominico's office in their home, I was surprised to find it filled with pictures of boats, and of himself and his friends on sailboats.

Yet, Luisa and her husband share a love of travel and camping. They travel in their camper to various parts of Europe and Africa. Their favorite trip was to Madagascar. They both enjoyed it immensely, as he was able to indulge his hobby of photography and she became intensely interested in the children whom she saw swarming in multitudes on the streets, begging and starving. She wanted to help them somehow.

After that trip they began to dream and plan how they might move to Madagascar. Luisa finally told her father what they were planning. He became furious and said that if she left Florence that he would take back all the money he had given them. She talked to him several times about their idea, each time coming away less sure of herself and her desire to move away. Her only consolation is that her husband has said that he is ready to give up his job and leave any time she is ready to go.

JULY 14

We have been here two weeks. Early this morning I heard someone singing outside. I opened the bedroom shutters to see our little gray-patterned landlady-farmer with her smiling voice washing clothes by the well below our window. I called out to her "Signora!" She stopped singing and slowly looked all around her. Then, when I called out again, she looked up and saw me with my as yet uncombed hair falling into my face, in the window and she smiled. I asked her if I could buy zucchini and fagioli (beans) and she said yes. So I took a bag and went barefoot down to the barn beneath us. She came in from the field with the young green zucchini and weighed them on her hand-held scale. She gave me more than a kilo`s worth and I carried them up the morning steps, feeling like they were loot won in battle. Inside the kitchen, my husband was already at the kitchen table "desk", where he writes from dawn to dusk every day.

He has been calmer and warmer towards me these last few days. He says he is writing a novel, a "pot-boiler" that he devised last week on the spur of the moment. Only twice has he come to the beach and sat, with his body almost as white as the sand, hoping to get a tan. He prefers to walk to town alone after I have taken the children ahead. On the beach he sat and smiled and joked with pretty Luisa for a short awhile before leaving and in the evening he sits peacefully, rather than stewing and taking long walks alone. On this "god-forsaken island" he feels he is being forced to sit and wait for the month to pass, but the sun, clean air and pretty women are restoring hope to his ever-despairing mind.

I see a different side of Luisa than my husband does. On the beach with her each day I see her controlling her children like puppets. They literally jump at her commands, which are most often commands that limit their freedom to enjoy the beach. They can only go into the water at certain times, and then only without clothes on, as the other Italian and German children do. After a half hour they must get out of the water and lie prone on the sand to warm up, swaddled in beach coats, whether they are cold or not. They can only use one aid to swimming, water wings, nothing else.

My children have inner tubes, which are forbidden to Luisa's children. But she belittles her children and prods them into swimming or doing things that they might normally be afraid to do. I let my children do or not do whatever is comfortable for them. They will grow up fast enough.

At meals, Luisa carefully controls her children's diet and they must eat every bit of what they are given. Every minute of their day is carefully scheduled ahead of time and no changes are allowed. They are rarely allowed to do things away from home, such as go to the movies, especially if someone might be smoking in the theater. Some of these things are traditionally Italian, but others are Luisa's own rules.

The boy, a handsome, blond lad, is nervous and giggling after he gets slapped by his mother for stepping out of line and subtly shows his hostility to others behind her back. The girl is silent and brooding, rarely smiling. But she is a robust, healthy little thing, preferring and excelling at sports and what might be called male activities in this gender-oriented society. She shows the restless strength and willpower of her mother and grandfather, but desires to be apart from others, like her father.

Luisa does not allow her desire to control everything stop

with her own family and extends it to mine whenever possible. She tells me what are the proper times and ways to do everything, especially where my children are concerned. She plans my daily activities, to the extent of supplying the means by which the activity will be carried out, from finding and arranging for this house we are renting to buying the proper type of sun lotion. For the most part I ignore any unwanted advice, but I have to admit that I am learning things and I take advantage of the good things she does for me and my family.

If her desire to work with children in Madagascar is real, I am beginning to wonder if it is only a desire to control other people's lives. Her alternative goal is to continue her schooling, completing her education in languages. She told her father that is what she wants, but he said he would only help her if she studied law so that she could become a partner with him in his law firm.

JULY 15

In the stuffy night, closed in against marauding mosquitoes, I lie in the darkness and listen to scratchy old songs on the radio: "Dixie" played in ragtime, "Oh, That Strawberry Roan," "Whoopee Ti-yi-yay," in Pete (Pay-tay) Seeger's familiar old voice. I hear the low voice of my husband coming from my daughters' room, as he tells them the story of Cain and Abel and peaceful Seth, a story from the beginning of history.

It occurs to me that Cain might have considered himself lucky at first, with the mark of protection on his forehead, when he was thrown out into the world outside of Eden. But I imagine that he began to miss home, becoming the first "Man without a country." He must have felt a deep sense of loss, knowing that he would never again hear a familiar language or practice the customs of his childhood, as he was forever banished. No easily understood sounds, no familiar gestures, no familiar routines; always doubting, always wondering whether what he was doing was correct, always being afraid of being misunderstood, always tripping over new words and ridiculed for his ignorance. It is difficult enough to find sympathetic tones in the words of your own land. And the words that come to the tongue in a foreign language are not always those that express one's exact meaning. It is difficult to seek communion of spirit in the words of a foreign language, unless one knows it well.

JULY 16

I am feeling sad and heavy with thought. My husband and I have been arguing. The tension I felt in him earlier this month is rising again, since Luisa is leaving the island soon. He seems calmer when she is around. I hate to compare myself with others, but I was forced to when my husband mentioned points about my personality that he did not like and which he admired in Luisa. It made me start looking at myself critically after his analytic comparison.

What is more, Luisa aroused memories of my parents in her long discussion about her relationship to her father today. To add more to think about, the English radio program tonight was about Librans, and I was surprised to find out how close to their description of Librans I am, always compromising, artistic and sensitive, yet having to be the peacemaker.

In his tirade, my husband claimed that I keep my feelings towards others inside, claiming my hostility, self-loathing and anger lie just beneath the surface. But I do not even know if I have these feelings he claims I have. When he forces me to see them, sometimes I recognize them in myself. As he pointed out during our argument today, it is true that I like to be alone, but the few times I am alone I usually do not turn my gaze inward in critical self-examination (though I am beginning to doubt myself right now).

Usually I enjoy being alone to create art or play music and when I am forced to be alone I feel the need to do these things. That means that something useful comes out of what I am and my reaction to what is around me. I am very sensitive to my surroundings.

As for anger, I accept everyone as being a good person, rather naively. If they do not accept me, it does not bother me much and I can usually block them out without too much trouble. If they try to provoke me, however, and I begin to feel anger towards them, it is true that I do not like to show my anger. I disguise it with polite smiles and words and by ignoring it. Only my husband can provoke me enough to lose my temper and leave the room furious, and he knows me well enough to be able to accomplish this.

Another thing about me that he mentioned was that I spend money too generously when I have it. But I like to see people happy. I buy presents when I have money and, on the positive side, when I do not have money I do not complain. Luisa, like my husband, is tight-fisted, counting every penny and worrying about where the next will come from before the first is spent.

I do not think my identity revolves around my wifely nor motherly duties as much as my husband would like it to, as Luisa's does, which he admires. I do not see my care of and duties toward my children or my husband as having much to do with my own identity. My world does not revolve around them, as Luisa's does. She must have told him she is devoted to her husband for him to mention this. But my husband and I have a completely different kind of relationship. He is one person, alone and autonomous, and I am a different person. He would like for me to be more dedicated to him, I guess, to build my world around him and hang on his every word. He thinks he would like this, but I think eventually it would gall him.

JULY 17

I am getting tan. My skin is darkening until I look like an Indian. My muscles are tightening with swimming a lot each day. I am thinner. I have always been petite, but I look and feel better with all this sun and exercise.

Last night I did not sleep well. The stuffy air clung to me

like moist moss, and I covered my face with the sheet against it, breathing only filtered air. The night was quiet and tense. Slight noises made me start awake whenever I would drift off. In the early morning the sun pierced through the shutters and the two layers of white, transparent curtains and shone onto my face. I arose and opened the windows to allow the fresh breeze in, but there was no breeze. For the first time, the morning wind did not billow the strips of light shining through the curtains around my feet. It usually fluffed the frail cloth into double images, the bars of light moving back and forth on the gauze. I opened all the shutters, looking for any sign of a breeze. But the air sat like a fat cat on the edge of the sill, stuffy and still, refusing to venture into the room. It languished on the top of the pear tree swelling with ripe, green balls. It would not even move to carry sounds of passing cars or beasts, only the muffled sounds of doves cooing in lazy burps, unexcited, unasleep, drowsing, complaining about the early heat.

The farmer's wife came toward me down the path which led from the plum tree, which had dropped its purple fruit in the yellow grass. Her handkerchiefed head was turned to the side, listening to the sound of her skirts billowing along the narrow path through the tall grass. She clutched in her left hand a bunch of ripe wheat, cut six inches from the head. It shone, swollen and golden in the sun. In her right hand she carried a sickle. Returning to the barn just below me, she was the picture of self-sufficiency, a bastion of independence born of necessity, harkening back to days long past for most of the world, when man and woman worked equally hard on farms to feed themselves with the food they grew.

Today they began stacking the hay which has lain for weeks in tidy bundles in the sun, turning from green to yellow. The black-hatted farmer led his gray donkey from bundle to bundle, loading it on the donkey's back until the load was bigger than the donkey. They walked down the dusty white road, tired man and patient beast, to the field where the hay is being piled. As the days go by, the pile will come to almost fill the field, becoming tall, square and yellow, like some great, golden temple. It will also be put into circular piles in the cattle lots, with a pole in the center, until it looks like a hut, each bundle leaning against the pole. A thick white top made of paper is spread over the highest point to keep the rain from going down the central pole through the hay and rotting it. As the year passes, the animals eat the bottom out of the piles in scallops, until it looks like an apple core.

After a morning at the beach and an afternoon of shopping

with Luisa I was tired. At home I found my oldest daughter ready and determined for me to pull out her loose tooth. I have to admire her. There is nothing she can not do in life if she puts her mind to it. She knows she will get 100 Lire from the tooth fairy and a package of candy from me if it comes out. I fastened a string to the tiny front tooth and began to pull. Her teeth are very firmly fastened in her head I found, even if they seem to be loose and wiggling. The last three teeth did not come out until the big teeth were already coming in. I pulled and pulled--giving jerks with her permission. She said it hurt, but there was no sign of blood or more loosening. Then I tied the string on a different way and it began to loosen. At the end of a half-hour she was crying and spitting blood and still not wanting to give up. But I finally gave up, and we went to sit on the back porch and rest.

She was shaking and leaned against her Dad, who came out to sit with us. The ordeal had worn her out and she went to sleep soon.

Marina di Campo

JULY 19

"He is very handsome, your husband." Luisa said to me, as we looked out over the countryside from our viewpoint on top the hill. Once, on the back of his picture, she had written the word "mafioso", which she told me meant "masculine." I have a strange sort of glee seeing him become attracted to my friend, whom he had disapproved of so in the beginning. He never likes my friends, but in this instance I was being proven right.

The wind was strong on the top of the hill Luisa and I had climbed. It overlooked the main port on the Island of Elba, Porto Ferraio. The rough rocks have been somewhat tamed by layer after layer of civilization, though they still looked rugged and impermeable from a distance. The city had blanketed the hills and the road, built by Napoleon in his boredom, efficiently easing the journeys between the little towns. The city laid below us was rusty orange, brown and dirty-looking, its fortresses the only neat thing about it, standing out against the blue of the ocean. Iron mines had made it and colored it (*See Notes at the end*). Napoleon, during his short stay, not only built roads, but developed laws to favor the mines. He also designed the flag of Elba still used today.

Luisa wore a native African dress, a long piece of cloth

wrapped around her body, twisted in the front with the ends tied around her neck, of bright red and white. She looked very attractive and comfortable. I felt less so in my knit slacks suit, which I rarely wear. This morning we two had come over the hills together in the bus, leaving the children with my husband and Luisa's mother. We were running off all by ourselves to explore the city. My husband had refused to come. He was more comfortable where he was, he said.

We found Napoleon's palace, a smallish one, appearing echoing and empty, in spite of the pale French Provincial furniture and white drapes, stained yellow in the sun, in the medium-sized rooms. It was poorly kept by some locals in uniform, who hounded us as we entered for a donation and then disappeared to loaf. The grass went uncut and the wooden walls needed painting. But you could imagine the pretence at majesty that must have been kept when Napoleon lived here in exile. He imposed his strong will and his powers of organization on this small and unwilling Italian population who had been happily neglected by European civilization for centuries, and who lived well through mining, fishing or growing grapes.

That Napoleon was thrust upon them without permission,

and that he used his overabundant organizational skills and willpower to whip them into shape, building roads, hospitals, civic buildings and forming a government, must have seemed to them a violation of their right to a little peace in life. A man used to governing the entire known world was bound to be rather demanding when he was given only a little island to govern. Below us on the hilltop we saw the distinct effect of his thwarted power: the bay cleanly outlined, the fortress jutting up enormous and well-designed, and the roads, still in good shape, extended in different directions from the center of the city to disappear over the hills.

Behind the city rose the mountains that ran through the center of the island. They formed two groups, the ones on the West end of the island and ones on the East. Our bus had climbed the hills between them, through the lowest point in the row that formed the backbone of the island, to go from Marino di Campo to Porto Ferraio. Tomorrow Luisa was going to leave the island and us, to travel back through the pass with her two children in her mother's chauffeured car. The driver would leave them at the ferry to the mainland. Once on the mainland, only faintly visible to us from this point on the island, they would take the train back to Florence.

As we stood looking at the view for the last time, we recalled the good times we had experienced together. I could not imagine Elba without Luisa. Her mother will stay on in the penthouse alone, until the season is over and the winds become too cold to tolerate. My family and I are staying another ten days, getting used to the idea of going back to the United States to live, now that we've gotten used to living in Italy.

It had been a lonely time in Italy for me until I met Luisa. She provided both friendship and the soothing sounds of English for me in what had seemed an alien land in spite of its warmth. For months I missed hearing English spoken and tried to learn Italian. Each night I struggled with the dictionary, searching it to find out what people had said to me during the day and using it to compose replies to them for the next day. It had been difficult at first. But as I learned the language, I felt as if I was relaxing and the city of Florence became beautiful to me in its familiarity.

Then I met Luisa. We both recalled how we met. We met on the public bus when I was going home one day, going up the hill past the Palazzo Pitti and Boboli Gardens on the bus which went all the way up to the Piazzali Michelangelo with the sculpture of his David overlooking the City of Florence below, beyond the

Arno River.

She is pure Italian, but when she heard me talking to my daughter, she struck up a conversation with me in perfect English. She loves to speak different languages and she wanted to practice speaking English. We both disembarked with all our children and packages at the same stop, half-way up the hill. To our surprise, we found that not only did we live across the street from each other, but we had children approximately the same age.

This was immediately seen as a benefit to us both. My children had no other English-speaking children to play with and she wanted her children to practice their English. That morning, when we parted on the street in front of our apartment building, she politely invited me to come to visit her and we went into our separate gates directly across the street. Her gate led to a large villa down a small road, at the end of which I had glimpsed beautiful landscaping and green lawns.

I politely responded that indeed I would come visit her, thinking I probably would never see her again. But that afternoon I heard the doorbell ring. When I ran down the stairs and opened the door, there stood Luisa. "Why didn't you come over to visit me?" She demanded, obviously irritated. I was flattered by her urgency.

She was so pretty, was about my age and seemed to like me. From that day on we saw each other almost every day. My children went to play in the villa gardens with hers, riding their bicycles or skating with her children's skates, and I enjoyed the hospitable spaciousness of the large, marble-floored villa rooms after the linoleum-carpeted rooms of our small apartment. And Luisa confided that she thought I was someone who could be a friend.

As summer approached, Luisa was torn between going with the children and camper alone somewhere or coming with me, my children and my husband (as we had nowhere else to go during that month) to Elba, where she had already arranged for us to rent a house. Her husband was going away for a month, but told her that he would not permit her to take the camper off by herself again, so it was decided that we all would go to Elba. At the last minute, Luisa's husband told her that she really should not go to Elba, as he had decided to remain at home and needed her to be there in the office to take care of him, his business calls while he was out, to do some selling for him and to keep the accounts, as she usually did.

She could not decide what to do. For a few days, every time I saw her she had a different plan; she had decided to go or to stay. But finally she bought the train and boat tickets for herself and her children a couple of days before my family was to leave for Elba and told her husband that she intended to take a vacation on Elba after all. As a compromise to him, however, she agreed to spend only three weeks on the island.

Now the time is up and tomorrow afternoon she is going back to Florence.

"I think that when I next write to you in the United States, I will be writing from Madagascar," she confided to me as we stood on the hilltop. "I do so want to go and help those poor little children. Their faces haunt me at night in my dreams." She spoke with only the trace of an Italian accent and with perfect English diction.

I looked at her, trying to imagine her helping children in Madagascar when her own two children preoccupied so much of her time. She had also talked about moving to the United States, but immigration to the U.S. was difficult and would take years.

Another problem with moving out of Italy was that they were only allowed to take so much money out of the country. She had described to me how she could bring money into Switzerland by hiding it in a sports car, which she would drive across the border. She had already asked my husband if he would take money out for her and he promptly told her he would not. I know that all this planning to escape is because she wants to remove her family from her father's domination. But she would be abandoning her mother, I thought.

We walked down the hill together, talking about immediate things, the weather, the flowers, the people, the houses, and the things she wanted to buy on our way back to the bus.

July 20

Luisa and her children spent their last morning on the beach with us. As we prepared to go home for lunch, my girls asked her children what they wanted to be when they grew up, while Luisa translated a few unfamiliar words for the children.

Her six-year-old son said he wanted to be a policeman. Her daughter at first said she wanted to drive a car. Then when Luisa explained that she meant "what profession", and gave the example of her father and grandfather (a salesman and a lawyer), the little girl replied a "doctoressa for children". Luisa was amazed. She evidently had not considered that her children might have their own goals; it had never occurred to her to ask them what they wanted to be.

I said good-bye to Luisa this afternoon in her and her mother's apartment, high above the beach. I really feel attached to her. She has been an unasked-for blessing, a very good friend on short acquaintance, someone who was working for my benefit from the moment I met her—such is her personality. She has taught me how to cook Italian food and introduced me to much in Italian culture. I helped her too, writing letters in English for her to the United States, painting portraits of her children for her and speaking in English with her almost every day since I met her. In spite of her nervous energy and the tremendous drive she possesses that makes her drive others around her, I like her. It may be that she is like me, as she says, in many ways.

When I got home this evening, I climbed up the back stairs to find the crab's shell had somehow fallen off the nail on the back porch and was lying crushed on the concrete floor. My husband was working alone in the kitchen as usual and the children were playing in the cool dining room.

JULY 21

I bought the tickets for our departure this morning. We

leave Elba in one week. Realizing this, I began to take on my old traveling attitude--that of existing on a different plane than reality, of just existing while changing environments.

In anticipation of the long trip back home, I began to look around me, savoring the last of this experience: the bright, direct sun, the noises, the odors, the heat, the dust, the water that I will not hear or smell or feel again. It becomes a series of pictures that I try to stuff into the various compartments of my brain. The bus stop at which I stand on the road, while waiting to go to town, the cars crowding past in the heat when I walk, the children playing on a yellow merry-go-round. I see it now. My baby climbs on, getting the new wet yellow paint on her fingernails, the corner nearby has a sign with Ma-Cel-Le-Ria on it, flipping in the wind down the front of the building. Inside is a handsome young butcher who smiles at me when I go in to buy meat. This familiar scene may disappear from my consciousness, because I will never see it again, and with time memories fade away.

Our house is in front of me now. I will describe it: a place of pain and comfort, the temporary living space we were given for a month above a barn. Dry, hot steps in front, going up into the kitchen. Clothes drying on the porch in only an hour in the hot wind. A green awning overhead to keep the sun out of the big kitchen, the cool interior dining room, dark and central, all doors opening into it. Our big, back bedroom, white and airy. The bathroom, small, pink and leaky. The girls' room, close, full of tiny toys underfoot, and gray bedspreads. When the windows are open the air blows through nicely through it all. I think I'll remember that—how refreshing the sweet-smelling ocean wind is on this hot, dry island.

My memories of places only recently in my past are colored by emotions, tiredness, our desire to return home, our lazy beach days and my little, dancing three-year-old baby running through it all. In Italy she was loved by all who saw her, with her blond-streaked hair, her cute baby face and blue eyes.

JULY 22

Some here on the island dread the coming of the sirocco winds from Africa. But to me they feel cool and refreshing after hot days with no wind at all. The winds have also brought warm currents, so bathing at the beach is very pleasant.

This evening at 7:00 my husband, the two girls and I set out to go to the top of the mountain that our house faces. We thought nothing of starting so late, since the days are now so long. I was dressed in slacks and cotton shirt, as was my oldest daughter. The three-year-old wore a pink dress, her hair in little pigtails. We all wore sandals. My husband was the only one really prepared for a hike, with comfortable shoes and heavy slacks. We should have dressed better because we eventually found ourselves threading between thistles and crown-of-thorn bushes.

We began by following the road up as high as we could, then discovering a well-trodden path beyond a patch of weeds at its end. It led uphill, weaving back and forth, near ancient terraces of grape fields, up dry stream beds and through high, grassy clearings. As we wound higher and higher, we were able to look back down at the valley gradually falling below us. The extremely clear air brought the tiny houses, the distant town and bay disappearing around the point, very close.

As we got near the top of the hill we felt the wind falling over the top of it from the sea on the other side—cool and fresh. Stopping to look back, we surveyed the valley, theatrically lighted by the evening sun, the trees casting long shadows over the fields. The bay lay flat, like a blue table with several tiny, white toy boats set up on it, all sitting still. The hills rose, shouldering their green bulk up out of the sea. Our eyes followed their heaves higher and higher until the great craggy bulk of raw rock split them and towered into the blue sky on the highest peak to our left.

Once more we thought that we were almost about to crest the top and be able to see over to the sea on the other side, which was our goal. But just short of the top we were thwarted by the wall of a carefully tended, terraced vineyard, cultivated up here in the wilderness, cut out of a hillside of tangled trees and bushes. Someone lived here. The path led along the side of the walled vineyard, up to a grove, within which we almost stumbled over a roughly assembled shack. Broken and abandoned bottles were piled in boxes or stacked near it. We exclaimed over our discovery, but were fearful to go any closer because it might be inhabited.

A tattered, red, beach umbrella spread its spokes near the front door, which was covered with bright strips of hanging plastic. The shack seemed made up of bits and pieces of other houses. The windows did not fit; the walls were constructed of various kinds of boards, plaster and rocks. It looked dirty and cluttered, but the ground around it was well-trampled, we noticed, meaning someone lived in it. We called out "hello?" but no-one answered. So we followed the path that led past the house, but it turned back downhill.

We had been walking for an hour and were ready to go home. We were tired, complaining and the sun was setting. We gladly followed a wider trail which we came upon that led in the general direction of our house. The dust had tracks showing us clearly that a donkey, a man and a dog had recently gone down it. Perhaps it was just as well that we had not met the hermit that lived in the shack—it was a big dog.

JULY 24

I saw Luisa's mother on the beach this morning, when the girls and I walked down to the end of the beach. We have been spending the mornings at a closer location to our road, now that Luisa has gone home. I waved at her and she seemed not to see us from under her big hat. Perhaps she had already drunk too much and was asleep, I thought. She sat as she always did, near her beach house, under the shade of her beach umbrella, but now she was alone.

We walked past and then turned and went back to our beach towels, now laid out among German families and their healthy, naked children. In the afternoon I finished the paintings of her grandchildren, which I will soon deliver to her to take back to Luisa when she returns to Florence.

JULY 25

We were up until midnight last night, having attended the Cinema where we saw Tatum O'Neal open her mouth and heard lots of Italian words come tumbling out, surprising us every time it happened. It was Paper Moon, a movie which, fortunately, we had seen twice in the U.S. so we knew the plot and the jokes, since there were no subtitles.

After the movie we walked home along our now-familiar road in the dark. A huge moon turned the little dirt road into pure silver, as it wound into the paper-cut-out trees. The air was so completely quiet and still, and the moon made the night so black and white, that it was like a still from the movie we had just seen.

Right now it is nap time. Since my seven-year-old was up late last night and did not get her prescribed ten hours of sleep, she is irritable and losing control of herself today. All I can do is close her in her room and make her take a nap in spite of her screaming that she does not want to. She is fighting sleep now, crying on her bed. But the youngest is sound asleep. She falls asleep wherever she is, when she gets tired.

Yesterday morning the old farmer borrowed his son's car, a Fiat, and drove us to the Western half of the island for special water from a spring he goes to. We drove along the road that winds over the sea cliffs, then along the coast through each little port town, finally arriving at the town located just across the narrow part of the island from here. The old man drove, with all five of us squeezed together, at full speed, careening around the curves, where we glimpsed rocks, jagged and bare, above us, vineyards neatly terraced beside us at times and brush-covered cliffs below us that slid into clear, azure waters. The tiny towns, all whitewashed, with terracotta roofs would appear suddenly as we rounded a hill. They cling to hillsides above tiny, perfect bays. At the inner lip of each bay the white sand spread out in a crescent where bathers and rows of bright umbrellas dot it with color. Far out to sea we saw the flat, black outline of Pianosa, the prison island, and the steep mountain of Monte Cristo arising bold and bare, out of the sea.

I think of the old movie, The Count of Monte Cristo, I once watched and knew why one would want to escape from it. The coast of Corsica lay beyond them, faintly seen behind the misty clouds that lay on the water, far out at sea.

As we circled huge Mount Carpanne that rises in the middle of this half of the island, we felt the fresh North winds that are characteristic of the northern side of the island. Pine forests, deep ravines, jagged rocks and healthy springs of water were glimpsed along the roadside. A feeling of typical Northwest crisp air, green trees, a smell of mint and flowers made that side of the island quite different from the soft, moist climate on the South where we live, where the hills are more yellow than green during the heat of summer.

The northern beaches are different, too. They do not contain white agate sand, but are made up of smooth, round river rocks, gray and black. Boats find deep harbors there and the mountains rise directly out of the water. The water here is dark blue and deep.

We stopped for spring water at a spot along the road outside of one of the little towns, helping Dino fill the big, empty wine bottles in his trunk. We came back home in a rush, taking the shorter route over the central saddleback to our two hot, sun-burnt houses, sighing when we finally stopped, still thinking of the cool mountains on the far side of the island.

Throughout the trip, the old farmer spoke in slurred Italian that I translated to my husband. He told us he is 66 years old and a grandfather, but his thick, strong body has no extra fat. He wore a light shirt and shorts. He was born and has always lived in Marino di Campo. I asked him if he had ever been away from Elba and he replied that he had moved one kilometer away from where he was born, in the town of Marino di Campo, with his family after he married, and built the house that we lived in.

Dino's new house, which he has recently built, is very tiny – just two rooms. However it looks as always looks as if twelve people live in it because there are grandchildren running in and out of it during the day, as he baby-sits. For a pastime he grows his grapes and makes wine. He lamented the new ways of people from the outside who come to the island and burn off the land so that it will be condemned and sold. The farmers are deserting the island, he said. Thousands of years of work, terracing the rich but rocky soil on the steep slopes and planting the slow-growing grapes vines, are destroyed overnight when the hills burn. Evidences of back-breaking hand labor from early times are seen all over the island, where, as far up as a mile above the ocean, terraces line the steep mountain sides. Small farmers working their own land and cultivating their small crops are finding it hard to remain on Elba. These days, on the hills, you see new white houses being built by wealthy Americans, Germans and Italians who, coveting the cheap land and seacoast of this Mediterranean Archipelago paradise, burn the old culture and build the new over it.

JULY 26

Today we played at being tourists, which was a lot of fun. My husband, suddenly on a generous binge, decided that we would all take the bus to Marciana, a tiny town high in the mountains, spectacularly set on the very top of a mountain peak, with only the jagged rocks of Mount Carpanne higher than it is and only a green-studded slope to the sea below it. It is an ancient town, its origins lost in time, impregnable and almost unreachable, except by a single road. Today the road is smooth and white, but I can imagine how the people were once able to fend off pirates and barbarians with ease on the steeps of what must have been a rugged trail up an untamed mountainside.

We walked up the steep steps into the town, once inside a barrier wall built by the Medici. There were no roads inside the wall, only walkways and stairs, the terrain is so steep. The dark, warm gray of the stone, glimpses of stairways on even higher levels above, bright and exotic flowers in window boxes or outside doors, the old painted, overpainted and repainted again facades of houses, with carefully stenciled ornamental designs around the doors, windows and corners of every house, are just part of the charming character of the mountain towns on the island.

But this town, larger and older than the others, had several good-sized piazzas, with natural springs flowing in fountains at their centers and benches and trees gracing their borders. At one level was a park with a war memorial dominating it, the sound of running water and cool breezes that scooped up the scent of mountainside mint, which enticed us to sit on benches and rest. There were green stretches of carefully planted lawns between a double row of trees. It reminded me of a road, shady and old, planted for the purpose of comforting the traveler in ages to come. Perhaps it had at one time been a road, for it led to a fort that had held off pirate invasions in the 1500's.

We sat for a quiet hour around a table for four in a sidewalk cafe. I was astonished that my husband would spend the money for lunch for the girls and me and actually take time to luxuriate in the atmosphere of a cafe after all his nervous financial warnings to me over the past month. I was animated and happy, enjoying the hour to its fullest while we each were served a delicious plate of spaghetti.

I sat looking across the table at my baby's sun-reddened, freckled face against the backdrop of blue ocean and green hills. Behind her an enormous begonia hung down its dewy, red head. A pot of geraniums sprouted beside her. On my right, my seven-year-old's smooth-skinned tan face with dark hair and dark eyes gazed in solemn absorption of the fantastic world around her. My husband sat to my left, almost relaxing, with a smile on his now-tanning face.

For the first time in three years he is being forced to relax and do nothing and it is good for him. Today he is not as anxious or tense as he usually is. His eyes are less red and wide open. His face is relaxed, he smiles more and takes time to do nothing. It is not like him, but I will enjoy it while it is here, whatever it means. He spent a long time playing and talking with the girls this morning. They are enjoying him too, like this.

JULY 27

I've developed a routine. As the sun begins to shine onto

my face through the lattices, I struggle awake, keeping one hand near my face to wave off the flies, who love to walk on me then. I prepare something—a breakfast—from nothing. My husband says we have very little money left. I am happy if I see two eggs and half a loaf of bread. So, if there is butter and jelly all of us can eat. The girls and I dress for the beach in bathing suits and carry our towels and toys. We walk the long, dusty, narrow road one more time, ready to give up our lives every time a car passes.

If my husband goes to the beach with us he walks (briskly, if he can in the heat) back and forth to town—something that wears me down, as I carry the bundles of clothes and food after swimming. I like to ride the bus or walk more slowly with the girls. So he walks at a different time, without us.

I swim out to the seca sand spit and back three times, doing the backstroke at least once. I lie in the sun. The girls play in the shallow water and the sand. We spend our small, allotted amount of money for lunch at some little grocery store buying bits of food, and buying bread at the bakery for a few pennies. The bread comes fresh from the ovens, where they have pulled it out on paddles. It cools in bins for awhile, then we tuck it under our arm, still warm and smelling like I imagine heaven does when and if I get there.

We walk the long walk back home in the sun at noon. After a cold drink of water in the shady kitchen, the children scatter to be by themselves. Lunch is gathered from the corners of the cabinets, our purchases in town and from plastic bags in the refrigerator. We sit down, willy-nilly, my husband joining us at the kitchen table. The flies join us to make it a crowd.

After lunch, the slow afternoon begins–sleep and quiet time for the children. It is a "doing-thing-I-haven't-had-time-for-yet" time for me, mending, cooking or washing.

After their naps, my oldest daughter tries to run off into the hot afternoon to play by herself, but her younger sister follows. Sometimes we girls go to the beach again or we all go someplace together. At supper time (as late as possible, but usually around 7:00) I bring out what I've hoarded from the other meals or bought during the day and try to make an edible meal out of it. Usually after the first couple of bites the girls try to leave the table. My husband eats dutifully, but makes an excuse to leave when I bring out the dessert, unless it is pastry or chocolate (preferably both). Following supper, after a few minutes of standing in the breeze of the porch, I herd, threaten, push, cajole and carry two little girls through two baths, two teeth-brushings, two good-night kisses, two drinks of water, two hushings and two assurances that they can swim tomorrow, before closing their bedroom door for good. Now I can read or write and finally sleep, at last. Late at night I feel very much alone in my own world.

Our nearing departure date is driving me to complete things for the trip. I bought a cheap, but colorful African rug and spent hours making a large bag from it to carry my larger paintings back to the United States. I am finishing up the paintings of Luisa's children, which I will give to her mother before we leave Elba.

Outside of the things I like to do, I move automatically to do the things I have to do, the right things, morning, noon and evening. I walk through them. They have become routine, yet I can not remember them. This morning is so far away that I do not recall the sound of water on the beach, the crunch of sand, the smell of the wind. I was there, but it is already gone, already a memory. The routine sweeps me on and already the light is fading on our trip. I don't even remember Luisa.

My husband is finally asleep, thank goodness. He has been so nervous. His eye is bothering him and he has headaches. He has not written anything lately. I think that is part of the problem. He is absolutely bored, but says he can not write. He is a tense, energetic person and very particular about what he does with his time. He does not swim. He only lies in the sun to get a tan when he goes to the beach.

He has nothing to do here at the house, so he lies on our bed or sits on the front steps, sometimes with a book, though he says he has already read every book in the house. He washes the clothes and dishes each day, but that does not take long. So he is bored and anxious, worrying about our trip back home because there's nothing else to worry about. He is always much calmer when he writes, and so am I, for though he is preoccupied with his manuscripts or about how to write something, at least what he is worried about does not concern me, and he is kept busy.

JULY 28

After I put the girls down for their nap today my husband and I had a fight that finally brought to a head all the worrying he has done lately over our trip and our finances. We were in the dining room and I was beginning to take things off the table. He mentioned that he was worried about one of the minor details that does not really concern him. He wanted me to leave the little, two-wheeled bag-toter in Florence and I want to keep it to pull one of my big bags with. I had also told him I wanted to take a bottle of Elban wine to our friends who are going to put us up in Connecticut for a couple of days when we arrive in the United States, but he will not let me buy any because he says we will have to pay taxes on it in customs.

I finally gave in to not buying the bottle of wine and said that I would consult him first on any purchases. But I resent this, and I reminded him that I have money budgeted to spend as I want and I do not think my small purchases from this fund should be approved by him. I point out to him that he never shows me the accounts, and that means I have no idea overall of how much money he has or how much he has budgeted for each item for our trip back.

Whenever he brings up my spending money, I remind him that he is not telling me what he is spending money for either. Besides, if he is worried about the fact that I want to carry things back to the United States, it will be me that is going to carry them, not him. I went on to say that because he controls the purse strings he can always call into question what I spend, but I can never question him and I never know how much money we have to spend, so cannot judge how much or how little to spend. It was the first time I had ever dared say that to him. In the past I have always done what he said to do without questioning him, though I resented it deeply at times.

He accused me of being unfair and spouting women's lib doctrine. He said he did not spend much (and I am sure he does not). He said he is very careful with money and never wastes it on buying drinks in town like another man might, or buying frivolous things. I said I was not criticizing him on how he spent his money, but only for not letting me know anything about how much we have or how he spends it.

At that point he got up, shoving his chair over in the process, grabbed his book, which he slammed onto the floor, and rushed away to get the money box, which was in the kitchen. He returned to the door of the dining room, fumbled with the cover of the box, scraped up the money that it contained and threw it all over the table and floor. He started throwing money at me and whacking me on the shoulder with his book, so I decided to leave the room.

But then he started talking. I paused and looked at him. His face was not red, it was white. "There, there's the money—you can see for yourself how much we've got. You manage it. You take over the accounts." He came toward me, so I escaped to the bedroom and locked the door. I heard him throwing my chair over and banging things around in the other room. He was kicking chairs, tables and knocking things off the tables. Then all was quiet.

I was determined not to cry. I stood at the window and looked out at the chickens calmly pecking in the dust and at the hot hills. I blew my nose. I looked in the mirror and told myself to be a man.

When I knew he was gone I cleaned up the broken things as best I could before the girls woke up, got the girls dressed when their nap was over and we walked to the beach. He would cool off, I told myself. When we came back at 7:00 he would be calm, but now I am upset.

That night as I bathed, he stood in the door to the bathroom and talked. The sound of the water half covered his voice, which I did not really want to hear. He gave me money. He explained the finances to me. He told me how mad I made him because I had such a “happy-go-lucky, I don't care" attitude about everything.

He knows this hurts me. I began to cry then, my hot tears streaming into the hot water. I told him that if my feeling that I did not care was a defense, it was my only defense. He said it was maddening to him. I said his actions were terrible to me. He said that they were his defense against me and that it would be better if I told him how I felt sometimes instead of not caring.

"If I don't care it's because if I cared it might hurt." The heat and the water were bracing me, now that my tears had been cried. "I don't like to hurt. I like the way I act and I'm not going to let people shove me around," I said with conviction.

At this he went and sat in the other room on the bed, but still watched me through the open door as I dried my hair and put oil on my body, a nightly ritual since I was in the sun so much.

"I'm sorry." I heard him say.

As suddenly as it had come, his anger had ceased. But my anger smolders now. I am sullen and thoughtful, as he refuses to discuss anything further, wondering when it will happen again.

JULY 30

The month is over and we are on a train, traveling out of Italy. Yesterday morning we all awoke before dawn and dressed. We gathered up our bags and began our last long walk to town, along the dim, deserted country road that wound through the side of the valley into the town. It was dawn. The sun had not yet come up over the hills to the East, but its first rays were already upon the slopes across the valley from us and lit up the small towns of Santo Piero and Sant'Ilario. The light showed us their distant facades, hugging the tops of their separate peaks as firmly as they had for centuries. Along the way we rested at a crossroad. The air was so clear that it looked as if we could reach out and touch the miniature towns on the mountain peaks around us.

We walked as fast as we could, carrying our heavy bags because my husband wanted us to reach the bus stop early. We reached town earlier than we had anticipated and set our bags down by the harbor wall to wait for the bus.

The town was quiet in the early dawn light. We four sat in a row on the wall, looking over the empty piazza at the sea. Beyond the narrow beach the boats sat on the smooth water, waiting for the tide. It was so still that they looked like a picture. When the sun finally began to come up over the hills, the water turned gold. The weather was cool and fresh. The beach was deserted, except for a lone figure far away, running with a romping dog.

Yesterday morning I had taken the two oil paintings of

Luisa's children to her mother. I was hoping to see her reaction to them, as I knew she appreciated art and loved her grandchildren very much. I took the elevator to the seventh floor. But when I rang the bell, only the maid came to the door. She said her mistress was not feeling well and asked what I wished to do. I told her I was leaving the paintings for her to take to Luisa, in Florence. She will return in a month or two, before the cold weather sets in, and rejoin her husband in the city of Florence.

Through the door, as the maid took the two canvases covered with paper, I glimpsed the shiny black polish of a grand piano, sitting in state in the living room. It had only a few pieces of music set up on it, with all of the covers closed. It must be true that she does not play it any more.

As the 7:00 hour approached, the little town began to awake. The gray taxi came to squat at the edge of the square. The driver got out and opened the taxi phone box to wait for calls, then leaned against his car. He spoke to the baker's wife on her way down the center of the street. A fisherman passed, heavy, slow and grizzled, dressed in navy blue sweatshirt and pants, black beret on his head and sandals on his feet. He looked at us curiously and we stared back, equally curious, until we shared embarrassment. Other travelers joined us, tensely awaiting the bus: two young German boys, a tanned, sophisticated woman and a farmer with a cheap summer suit and fat suitcase. The air was stiff with anticipation of the bus' arrival.

When it arrived we piled on with our bags. It took us on our final trip over the saddleback. In PortoFerraio we caught the ferry and began to sail across the surface of the cold, dark water at midday, through the sun, turning so we went around the tiny rock islands bordering the larger island. At the town of Cavo, Elba, we drew near to the rocks and a small boat put out from the dock to meet us. Passengers jumped across the churning water onto the metal ladder dropped down the side of the larger boat. Their bags were handed across by men in white t-shirts with "Naval Italia" written across the fronts.

From Cavo we set out to cross the body of water that had separated us from mainland Italy for a month. It was a windy trip, sunny and strangely joyful. As we arrived in Piombino, on the mainland, it seemed like a huge crowd of people had gathered on the pier to meet us. But they were only waiting for the ferry's return trip to Elba. We set foot on the mainland with sadness and a tinge of relief. We were nearing the end of our stay in Italy.

We caught a train to bear us out of the country, away from the sea that still sparkles, the beach where old friends return to sit and chat on the white sand, carrying us away from little farms in hot valleys that have grown lush grapes, fruits, wheat and vegetables every summer for centuries and probably will for centuries to come.

POST SCRIPT

Luisa finally wrote a long letter to me about her mother after I returned to the States. When Luisa left Elba her mother appeared to all eyes to be in good spirits for as long as she was on the island, but according to her friends, she grew thinner and quieter as the days drew near to her return trip to Florence. At the end of the summer, the day before her husband was to join her to take her back to Florence, she leaped from the balcony of the penthouse. The building was seven stories high.

Back in Florence, Luisa was shattered by the news of her mother's death. She told her children only that "Grandmamma has gone to live in heaven," and took to her bed. She stayed in bed for three months, refusing to eat, with the blinds drawn, refusing to see anyone, not even her own family members. At last she arose and began to plan her escape from Italy as she had dreamed of doing.

Within the year, she, her husband and children emigrated to Australia. They had sold their house and furniture in Florence as quickly as they could and left. After that last letter from her, sent from somewhere in Australia, there has only been silence.

ELBA JOURNAL

NOTES ON ELBA

MON ILE EST BIEN PETITE

There are seven islands in the Tuscan Archipelago: Elba, Capraia, Giannutri, Gorgona, Giglio, Pianosa and. Montecristo The largest of them is Elba (223,5 square kilometers). The Medici family in Florence, Italy, built the walls of Portoferraio and developed the culture of Tuscany on Elba.

Elba has a long history dating back to the Etruscan iron mines in the eighth century B.C. The iron mines of Elba furnished ore to the Roman Empire in large quantities, and these same mines continued to produce iron and other valuable natural products until the 1980's. Five centuries ago the Etruscans dominated the island, building various necropolises and blast furnaces for the iron they mined, as well as structures in and for surrounding villages. The Etruscans and Romans mined and processed local haematite and limonite, as well as iron.

The Romans also appreciated the mud baths of Elba, leaving two patrician villas with thermal structures. In the Middle Ages, domination by the Pisans left buildings used in defense of the area, showing how important and valuable the island was. Cosimo De' Medici and the Seignory of the Appiani also ruled the island. Cosimo built a town called Cosmopoli (now called Portoferraio) and built walls around it on top of what had been a Roman Fabricia, to protect the island from pirate raids.

Elba's iron mines are on the eastern coast, Terra Nera and Capo Bianco, to the north-east of Porto Azzurro; there was also mining of pyrite, haematite and magnetite. The Ortano mine is north of Ortano beach, from which pyrite was used to produce sulphuric acid. Huge crystals of hedembergite and ilvaite crystals were found in here. The Rio Marina mine produced huge quantities of haematite and pyrite. The town of Rio Marino contains the Mineral Museum, which exhibits more than 700 kinds of rare and beautiful minerals.

Rich in minerals, the soil of Elba produces a botanical garden of fantastic flora and fauna. An enormous variety of fish, dolphins, birds, and butterflies co-exist here. On restaurant menus the fare not only includes fresh vegetables and fruit, but the island is also known for its delicious Porcini mushrooms, risotto and octopus cacciatore.

The island measures about 20 by 30 km, but is two quite separate mineral localities. In the west and center, the Monte Capanne pluton produces monzonitic pegmatites and granitic formations within which crystal specimens of orthoclase, elbaite, spessartine, beryl, pollucite petalite, and other pegmatitic crystals may be found. On the eastern coast the deposits of hematitic iron ore produces world-famous specimens of ilvaite, pyrite, hematite, native copper, and other copper species.

Quoting from NAPOLEON BANISHED, The Journeys to Elba and to St. Helena Recorded in the Letters and Journal of two British naval officers: Captain Thomas Ussher and Lieutenant Nelson Mills (in 1814), published in 1955 in England:

> *The first days of Napoleon's banishment to the Island of Elba is recorded by Captain Ussher. He is first greeted by the islanders as he disembarks the H.M.S. Undaunted:*
>
> *. . .On the beach he was received by the mayor, municipality and the authorities, civil and military. The keys were presented on a plate, and the people seemed to receive him with great welcome, and shouts of 'Vive l'Empereur!' We proceeded to the church in procession; thence to the Hotel de Ville, where all the authorities and principal inhabitants assembled, with each of whom he conversed. After that he mounted his horse, attended by a dozen persons, and visited part of the outworks and dined at seven o' clock.*
>
> *Next morning he was up at four, and from that until ten was on foot visiting the fortifications, storehouses, magazines, etc. At two he mounted his horse, and I rode with him about two leagues into the country, over mountains and precipices, but nothing is impassable to him. He examined the country houses, and stopped at a planter's (wine merchant) and had a cold collation. He helped me to different things, which he never does to any one else. A lady came in and offered him strawberries, which he gave to me. I took an opportunity afterwards of offering him a sprig of laurel, which pleased him much. He asked me here how I liked the wine. I said it was excellent; and he immediately ordered 2000 bottles to be sent on board to the men. In short, his manner is always most agreeable and polite, and it's only when anxious to carry any point that he is passionate.*

Next day we went across the island to a mountain of iron, the richest and finest mine in the world--and, what is remarkable, the revenue arising from it formerly paid his Legion of Honour. We rode through the clouds to it. I never was so fatigued in my life. The mountain is completely of iron, and is blasted with powder in the way that quarries are in England. When broken, the fragments are like pieces of diamond, of all colours. He gave me some beautiful specimens of his collection. . . .

We afterwards went through a labyrinth to a high mountain, upon the summit of which there is a temple erected by the Romans in honour of Jupiter. I suppose he consulted the oracle. At dinner we had a boar's head, and the Emperor with his usual kindness to me helped me to the eye as a great treat. I was hard set what to do. It was rudeness to refuse, but I could not stand it, and sent it away; the very idea spoiled my appetite.

Elba is a beautiful island, possessing every advantage. The bay of Porto Ferrajo is unrivaled and the valleys are uncommonly fertile, yielding the finest vegetables of every description, and the mountains are to the summits clothed with vines. In three or four days he visited every part of the island, conceived all his plans for building palaces, stables, aqueducts, lazarettos,[public hospitals] etc. (The latter he begged I would plan.)

The day that he was on the summit of a mountain that showed him all the island, he turned round laughing and said, "Ah! mon ile est bien petite.'

www.ingramcontent.com/pod-product-compliance
Lightning Source LLC
LaVergne TN
LVHW020651100826
845148LV00012B/2430

* 9 7 8 0 9 8 1 8 4 4 2 2 0 *